The Canterville Ghost

Text adaptation and activities
by Gaia Ierace

Contents

Design and Art Direction: Nadia Maestri
Layout: Sara Blasigh

© 1999 Black Cat Publishing,

We would be happy to receive your comments and suggestions,
and give you any other information concerning our material.
info@blackcat-cideb.com
blackcat-cideb.com

The Publisher is certified by

 CISQCERT

in compliance with the UNI EN ISO 9001:2008
standards for the activities of 'Design, production,
distribution and sale of publishing products.'
(certificate no. 04.953)

ISBN 978-88-7754-520-6

Printed in Italy by Stamperia Artistica Nazionale, Trofarello, Turin

Pictionary 1

stars   stripes

dining room

'Superwhite'

twins

red stain

living room

fireplace

milk

sugar

tea

CHAPTER 1

England welcomes the Americans

Mrs Umney: Good afternoon Mr Otis, Mrs Otis.
Come in! Lord Canterville is in the dining room.

Butler: Mrs Umney, Lord Canterville is not in the
dining room.

Mrs Umney: Where is he?

Butler: He's in the red living room.

Lord Canterville: Welcome to my home Mr and Mrs Otis.

Mr Otis: This is my daughter Virginia and these are the twins, Stars and Stripes. This is my other son, Washington.

Lord Canterville: Good afternoon. Please sit down.

Mr Otis: Thank you sir.

Lord Canterville: Some tea, Mrs Otis?

Mr Otis: Yes, please.

Lord Canterville: Milk?

Mr Otis: Yes, please.

Lord Canterville: Some tea, Virginia?

Virginia: Thank you, Lord Canterville.

Lord Canterville: Sugar?

Virginia: Two, please.

Lord Canterville: Here you are.

Lord Canterville: Do you like Canterville Chase, Mr Otis?

Mr Otis: Yes, I do. Canterville Chase is a perfect home for us.

Stars: Yes! It's perfect!

Lord Canterville: I'm very happy but... you know about the ghost of course!

Mr and Mrs Otis: A ghost...?

Lord Canterville: Yes, an old ghost.

Mr Otis: Is he English?

Lord Canterville: Of course, madam. He was an English aristocrat.

Lord Canterville: Look at the red stain near the fireplace. The ghost stains the floor every night.

Washington: Is it blood?

Lord Canterville: Well, Mrs Umney cleans the stain every day but every morning the stain is there again.

Mr Otis: I'm sure 'Superwhite' can clean it! We want the house and the ghost.

Lord Canterville: So does that mean...?

Mr Otis: ...Yes!

Lord Canterville: Jolly good! Welcome to England!

1 Choose the correct answer.

1 Lord Canterville is in
  A ☐ the red living room.
  B ☐ the green living room.
  C ☐ the dining room.

2 Mr and Mrs Otis have
  A ☐ two children.
  B ☐ three children.
  C ☐ four children.

3 The names of the twins are
  A ☐ Milk and Sugar.
  B ☐ Stars and Stripes.
  C ☐ England and America.

4 At Canterville Chase there is
  A ☐ an American ghost.
  B ☐ an English ghost.
  C ☐ an Italian ghost.

5 The stain is
  A ☐ pink.
  B ☐ green.
  C ☐ red.

2 Match the pictures with the words.

a ghost

a stain

a fireplace

a star

a house

3 Act the story.

STUDENT A: You are Mrs Umney

STUDENT B: You are the Butler

STUDENT C: You are Lord Canterville

STUDENT D: You are Mr Otis

STUDENT E: You are Mrs Otis

STUDENT F: You are Virginia

STUDENT G: You are Stars

STUDENT H: You are Washington

Pictionary 2

attic

love

noise =
Crash! Bang!

hate

soap

dirty

CHAPTER 2

The Americans at Canterville Chase

Mrs Umney: Good morning, Mr and Mrs Otis.

Mrs Otis: Good morning, Mrs Umney. Can you show us the house please?

Mrs Umney: Yes, of course. Let's go upstairs.

Mrs Umney: This is the attic.

Washington: It's ideal for ghosts.

Mrs Otis: Yes, ghosts love attics.

Mr Otis: It's dirty. Here's 'Superwhite', Mrs Umney. This will clean it. It's very good.

Mrs Umney: Yes, sir.

Mr Otis: What's that?

Virginia: I think it's our ghost.

Mr Otis: Time to go to bed, kids. It's late!

Mrs Otis: Goodnight, sweet dreams.

Stripes: Goodnight, Dad.

Stars: Goodnight, Mum.

Stripes: What's that noise downstairs?

Stars: Let's go and see!

Stripes: Look, here's the ghost!

Mr Ghost: Red stains, red stains... I like red stains!

Stars: It isn't a white ghost!

Stripes: Of course not. Not all ghosts are white!

Stars: Oh yes. American ghosts have red stripes and white stars.

Mr Ghost: Who's there?

Stripes: Hello, Mr Ghost. My name is Stripes Otis and this is my twin brother Stars Otis.

Mr Ghost: You are scared, aren't you?

Stars: Of course not. We love old, English ghosts.

Stars: Hello Virginia. This is Mr Ghost.

Virginia: Hello sir. My name is Virginia Otis.
I like the stain.

Stripes: Our dad hates stains. He loves
'Superwhite'.

Mr Ghost: What's 'Superwhite'?

Virginia: It's soap. It's American.

Mr Ghost: It's late. I must go. Goodbye.

1 Choose the correct answer.

1 Ghosts love
- **A** ☐ homes.
- **B** ☐ gardens.
- **C** ☐ attics.

2 American ghosts have
- **A** ☐ black stars.
- **B** ☐ white stars.
- **C** ☐ red stars.

3 The twins love
- **A** ☐ French ghosts.
- **B** ☐ Italian ghosts.
- **C** ☐ English ghosts.

4 Mr Otis hates
- **A** ☐ ghosts.
- **B** ☐ stains.
- **C** ☐ children.

5 'Superwhite' is
- **A** ☐ soap.
- **B** ☐ tea.
- **C** ☐ sugar.

2 **Find the six words in the box and circle them.**
   Then match them with the pictures.

A M E R I C A W J H U O
H E D Y H S T R I P E S
B F G B R T T W I N S M
N O I S E J N H Y H F Y
K J S U P E R W H I T E
M J M C L O C K J U J D

3 **Act the story.**

STUDENT A: You are Mrs Umney

STUDENT B: You are Mrs Otis

STUDENT C: You are Washington

STUDENT D: You are Mr Otis

STUDENT E: You are Virginia

STUDENT F: You are Stripes

STUDENT G: You are Stars

STUDENT H: You are Mr Ghost

Pictionary 3

Sun Oil

chains

white sheet

boots

roast beef and potatoes

Windsor Castle

CHAPTER 3

Mr Ghost:
the end of a glorious career

Mr Otis: What's that?

Mrs Otis: It's a terrible noise. It's the ghost. Give him the Sun Oil!

Mr Otis: My dear sir, you need some oil for your chains. Use the Sun Oil! Sun Oil is perfect for your chains.

Mr Ghost: This is a terrible insult for a ghost!
It's the first time after a glorious career of three
hundred years. Why can't I scare the Americans?

Mr Ghost: What's that? It's a horrible, white ghost.

THE OTIS' GHOST

THE ONLY TRUE AND ORIGINAL GHOST

but... but it's only a white sheet!

Children have no respect for old ghosts.

From now on, I promise to:

- REMOVE MY BOOTS
- BE SILENT
- USE THE SUN OIL FOR MY CHAINS

Virginia: Are you sad Mr Ghost? My brothers are going back to Eton tomorrow. We promise to be nice to you, but you must promise to be good.

Mr Ghost: I can't be good. I'm a ghost. I must rattle my chains, I must walk at night, I must moan.

Virginia: Calm down, Mr Ghost.

Virginia: You are very bad! First you take all my colours to paint your stain. First the red, then the green and the yellow. I can't paint any more. It's so sad!

Mr Otis: Virginia!

Virginia: Yes, Dad?

Mr Otis: Dinner is ready.

Virginia: I must go.

Mr Ghost: Goodbye, Miss Virginia!

Mrs Umney: Do you want some more roast beef and potatoes?

Washington: Yes, please.

Mr Otis: Are you happy to go back to Eton, Washington?

Washington: Yes, dad. I like it near Windsor Castle.

Stars: I like it too.

Stripes: Me too!

1 Choose the correct answer.

1 The Sun Oil is
- **A** ☐ perfect for animals.
- **B** ☐ perfect for stains.
- **C** ☐ perfect for chains.

2 Mr Ghost has a long career of
- **A** ☐ 300 years.
- **B** ☐ 200 years.
- **C** ☐ 350 years.

3 The Otis' ghost is
- **A** ☐ blue.
- **B** ☐ red.
- **C** ☐ white.

4 Mr Ghost has got
- **A** ☐ chains.
- **B** ☐ shoes.
- **C** ☐ tea.

5 Eton is near
- **A** ☐ Rome.
- **B** ☐ Windsor Castle.
- **C** ☐ New York.

Match the pictures with the words.
Now listen to the noises and write the number next to the picture.

| the wind | chains | the clock | ghosts |

a. ☐ ....

b. ☐ ....

c. ☐ ....

d. ☐ ....

3 Act the story.

STUDENT A: You are Mr Otis

STUDENT B: You are Mrs Otis

STUDENT C: You are Mr Ghost

STUDENT D: You are Virginia

STUDENT E: You are Mrs Umney

STUDENT F: You are Washington

STUDENT G: You are Stars

STUDENT H: You are Stripes

Pictionary 4

dark / light

sun

storm = rain /
thunder / lightning

garden: blue, pink,
white flowers

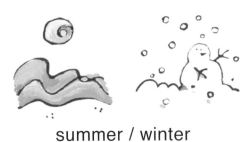

summer / winter

birds

CHAPTER 4
Sir Simon's world

Mr Ghost: Miss Virginia, Miss Virginia, wake up!

Virginia: Who's that?

Mr Ghost: It's me!

Virginia: Hello Mr Ghost. What are you doing here? It's late. Aren't you tired?

Mr Ghost: Yes, Miss Virginia but I can't sleep.

Virginia: That's terrible. Sit down! What's your real name?

Mr Ghost: It's Sir Simon de Canterville.

Virginia: Listen! What's that?

Mr Ghost: It's a storm... can you hear the rain and thunder and see the lightning?

Virginia: It's so dark! Do you like the dark?

Mr Ghost: Well, Miss Virginia, ghosts live in the dark.

Virginia: I prefer the light and the sun. I love summer.

Mr Ghost: In my world it's winter all the time.

Virginia: Poor, poor ghost. It's so sad.

Virginia: Don't cry, Sir Simon! Can I help you?

Mr Ghost: I'm so tired. I want to sleep.

Virginia: Is there a place where you can sleep?

Mr Ghost: Yes, there is.

Virginia: Where is it?

Mr Ghost: It's a little garden with blue, pink and white flowers. Birds sing there day and night.

Virginia: Can we go there?

Mr Ghost: Children can't go there, but they can cry for ghosts.

Virginia: I can cry for you, Sir Simon.

Mr Ghost: Can you dear?

Virginia: Good morning, Mum.

Mrs Otis: Are you OK, dear?

Virginia: Yes, Mum. What time is it?

Mrs Otis: It's ten o'clock. It's late!

Virginia: Where are the twins and Washington?

Mrs Otis: Outside. They are ready to go to Windsor.

Washington: Bye, Mum and Dad. Bye, Virginia. Come to visit us in Windsor.

Virginia: Yes, alright. I'll come next summer.

Mrs Umney: Goodbye, boys. Take care!

Washington: Goodbye, Mrs Umney. Here's some 'Superwhite' for you.

Mrs Umney: Thank you, Washington.

Everybody: Goodbye.

1 Choose the correct answer.

1 Mr Ghost's real name is

A ☐ Sir Henry.

B ☐ Sir John.

C ☐ Sir Simon.

2 This is ⚡⚡

A ☐ rain.

B ☐ lightning.

C ☐ a stain.

3 Virginia loves

A ☐ the dark.

B ☐ summer.

C ☐ winter.

4 In the garden there are

A ☐ blue, pink and white flowers.

B ☐ white and red flowers.

C ☐ green and yellow flowers.

5 Virginia can

A ☐ cry for Mr Ghost.

B ☐ sing to Mr Ghost.

C ☐ play tennis with Mr Ghost.

2 **Make your ghost mask.**

You need: a large white paper bag – crayons –

scissors

 **1** Draw the eyes, nose and mouth on the paper bag.

2 Cut out the eyes and mouth and colour the mask.

 **3** Put on your mask.

Let's play!

Ask your school-friends: 'Who am I?' When they guess, remove your mask. The last person to wear the mask is the winner. Good luck!

3 **Act the story.**

STUDENT A: You are Mr Ghost

STUDENT B: You are Virginia

STUDENT C: You are Mrs Otis

STUDENT D: You are Washington

STUDENT E: You are Mrs Umney

STUDENT F: You are Mr Otis

STUDENT G: You are Stars

STUDENT H: You are Stripes

Pictionary 5

church

ancestor

fairies

witches

elves

CHAPTER 5
Goodbye Sir Simon!

Mr Otis: Ladies and gentlemen, welcome to my church.

Mrs Otis: Come here, Virginia. This is the Duke of Canterville.

Virginia: Good morning, Duke.

The Duke: My name is Cecil.

Mrs Otis: Let's go, Duke Canterville! Lunch is ready.

The Duke: Thank you, Mrs Otis.

The Duke: Do you like Canterville Chase, Mrs Otis?

Mrs Otis: Yes, we all like it. Virginia loves England.

The Duke: What about the ghost? Is he quiet now?

Mr Otis: Oh yes. He's very quiet because he oils his chains. He doesn't visit us very often.

Mrs Otis: And there's no stain now!

The Duke: Jolly good!

The Duke: Is England different from America?

Virginia: Oh, yes! Very different. America is a big country and it's new! But England is full of history!

The Duke: And ghosts!

Virginia: I like ghosts. Our ghost is a gentleman!

The Duke: Is he? I know he walks at night in the dark. He moans and his chains make a terrible noise.

Virginia: This is only part of his story! He's a very sad ghost. He can't sleep.

The Duke: Sir Simon is my ancestor. He's over 300 years old.

Virginia: He's very old!

The Duke: In England we have ghosts and fairies and elves. They live in the woods.

Virginia: In America we have witches. They live in forests and they prepare magic herbs.

Virginia: Look at the flowers, Cecil! I love blue, pink and white flowers.

The Duke: Do you like white roses?

Virginia: Yes, I do.

The Duke: This is for you, Virginia.

Virginia: Thank you, Cecil. It's lovely.

Mr Ghost: Virginia, Virginia, I'm happy because you cry for me. I can sleep now.

Virginia: Where are you?

Mr Ghost: In the garden. Miss Virginia, this box is for you.

Virginia: Oh, look at the diamond ring and the earrings. They're beautiful! Thank you, Sir Simon. Goodbye!

1 Choose the correct answer.

1 The Duke's name is
A ☐ Frank.
B ☐ George.
C ☐ Cecil.

2 Fairies live in
A ☐ America.
B ☐ England.
C ☐ Australia.

3 Witches prepare
A ☐ roast beef.
B ☐ magic herbs.
C ☐ tea.

4 Virginia likes
A ☐ white roses.
B ☐ yellow roses.
C ☐ red roses.

5 Sir Simon gives Virginia
A ☐ colours.
B ☐ white roses.
C ☐ a diamond ring and earrings.

2 Listen and write the number next to the right picture.

3 Act the story.

STUDENT A: You are Mr Otis

STUDENT B: You are Mrs Otis

STUDENT C: You are Virginia

STUDENT D: You are the Duke

STUDENT E: You are Mr Ghost

Mr Ghost's song

Look at the song and match each letter with the right number.

A ☐ Welcome to Canterville Chase
With Mr Ghost in his chains
Can you hear the rattle in the dark
Over there, in the park?

B ☐ The clock strikes five
One Two Three Four Five

C ☐ Look! Here's a stain
As red as fire
Red stains   Red stains
I like red stains
Upstairs   Downstairs

D ☐ Good morning Mr Otis
Be quiet, Mr Ghost
Sun Oil, Superwhite...
Ssshh!   Be quiet!

E ☐ Good morning sweet Virginia
This is for you
And...
Thank you!

Copy the song into your notebook and draw the ghost.